W9-AEH-243

GROUNDBREAKERS

Sir Francis Drake

Neil Champion

Heinemann Library
Chicago, Illinois

© 2001 Reed Educational & Professional Publishing
Published by Heinemann Library,
an imprint of Reed Educational & Professional Publishing,
Chicago, Illinois
Customer Service 888-454-2279
Visit our website at www.heinemannlibrary.com

Designed by AMR
Illustrated by Art Construction
Originated by Ambassador Litho Ltd.
Printed in Hong Kong by Wing King Tong

05 04 03 02 01
10 9 8 7 6 5 4 3 2 1

Library of Congress Cataloging-in-Publication Data
Champion, Neil.
    Sir Francis Drake / Neil Champion.
        p. cm. -- (Groundbreakers)
    Includes bibliographical references (p.) and index.
    ISBN 1-58810-048-0 (library binding)
    1. Drake, Francis, Sir, 1540?-1596--Juvenile literature. 2. Great Britain--History,
Naval--Tudors, 1485-1603--Juvenile literature. 3. America--Discovery and
exploration--English--Juvenile literature. 4. Admirals--Great
Britain--Biography--Juvenile literature. 5. Explorers--America--Biography--Juvenile
literature. [1. Drake, Francis, Sir, 1540?-1596. 2. Explorers. 3. Admirals.] I. Title. II.
Series.

DA86.22.D7 C47 2001
942.05'5'092--dc21
[B]
                                                                    00-058145

Acknowledgments
The author and publishers are grateful to the following for permission to reproduce copyright
material: Bridgeman Art Library, pp. 11, 16, 17, 29; British Library Reproductions, p. 40;
Huntington Museum, p. 23; J. Allan Cash Ltd, pp. 10, 30; James Davis Travel, pp. 21, 37; Mary
Evans Picture Library, pp. 15, 19, 33; Michael Holford, p. 34; National Maritime Museum, pp. 4,
8, 9, 13, 31, 32, 35; National Portrait Gallery Picture Library, pp. 26, 36; Ossie Palmer, pp. 6, 24;
Panos Pictures, pp. 18 (Marcus Rose), 25 (Jeremy Horner), 38 (Jeremy Horner), 39 (Jon
Mitchell); Plymouth City Museum, p. 41; Public Record Office, p. 5; South American Pictures, p.
28 (Sue Mann); The Art Archive, pp. 14, 20, 27.

Cover photograph reproduced with permission of the National Portrait Gallery.

Some words are shown in bold, **like this.** You can find out what
they mean by looking in the glossary.

Contents

The Man and the Myth

Sir Francis Drake is pictured here at the height of his fame and fortune. He became an influential figure in matters to do with the sea and the navy.

Sir Francis Drake (1540?–1596) is one of the great heroes of English seafaring history. He is seen as the typical swashbuckling, brave, patriotic, noble rogue. Drake went to sea in his teens to make his fortune as a **pirate** and ended up as a vice admiral commanding a fleet on behalf of his queen. He fought for the influence and power of England, and for the **Protestant** religion, about which he was passionate.

Pirate to a queen

How did Drake move from being a pirate, robbing Spanish ships and bringing treasure back from South America, to becoming the person we associate with the defeat of the **Spanish Armada** and the defense of the Protestant faith against the **Catholic** nations of Europe? We know that he was the second person in history to sail around the globe, and the first European to land off the coast of what is now California, claiming that land for Elizabeth I of England. But around such facts, legends have inevitably grown.

Finding the truth

The problem we have today is that of separating the myth from the reality. Because he became a national hero in his own lifetime, everything written about him from that period needs to be examined closely.

Stories told by and about Drake became exaggerated. Sometimes his actions were reported in the best light—a "spin" was put on them to show him as he wanted to be seen: strong, **patriotic,** noble, and daring. He was all these things, but he was also greedy, ruthless, self-serving and, on occasions, cowardly.

Lack of information

Anyone looking at the life of Sir Francis Drake has to accept that, because he lived over 400 years ago, there are gaps in our knowledge. People in Elizabethan England kept some records, such as **parish registers, wills,** records of important events, royal letters and orders, personal letters, ships' **logs,** and so on, but these do not give us a complete picture of a life. However, we do know enough to give us an impression of Drake and the Elizabethan England into which he was born.

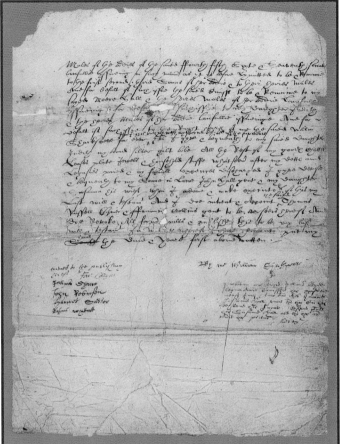

The will of William Shakespeare, who lived at about the same time as Drake. Parish registers and wills are some of the few documents that tell us something about 15th-century English society.

THE AGE OF EXPLORATION

Drake was an explorer. During his lifetime, European geographical knowledge was expanding faster than ever before. People from Europe sailed to many new lands, including North and South America, India, the Spice Islands—even the frozen wastelands of Greenland and Canada. They went looking for trade, treasure, and new lands that their countries could colonize. Spain and Portugal were the most successful early on, but countries like England and France eventually caught up.

A Devonshire Farm Boy

Sir Francis Drake was born near Tavistock in the county of Devon. The nearest important town was Plymouth, a port on the south coast of England. We do not know exactly when he was born, because the records of the time are unclear, but it was between 1536 and 1546—probably around 1540. His father was named Edmund Drake; his mother may have been Anna Myllwaye, but we cannot be sure. He was the eldest son of what seems to have been a very large family—twelve sons by one account!

The Drake family

For several generations, the Drake family had been farming at Crowndale—a mile or so southwest of Tavistock. They did not own their land, but leased (rented) it from Tavistock Abbey, and were reasonably well off. When the monasteries and abbeys were **dissolved** by Henry VIII, the king gave the lands to one of his nobles, Lord Russell. Lord Russell continued leasing the land to farmers like the Drakes, but not on such good terms.

The ruins of Tavistock Abbey are pictured here. Once a large and thriving community of monks lived and prayed there.

Family history

Drake's grandparents were John and Margerie. They had three sons, John, Edmund, and Robert. As was the custom at the time, the eldest son would inherit the farm, so Drake's father had to find his own career. He chose to become a **Protestant** vicar, moving to Kent—the other side of the country. Edmund taught his sons to read and write, but we do not know what other education they received. Francis started working at a very young age, while living with his father in Kent. He worked on the boats that went up and down the Medway River, the Thames, and the English Channel, and began to learn his seafaring trade. But it was in the west, back in Devon, that his training really began.

The map shows part of the counties of Cornwall and Devon in southwest England, where Drake was born and spent much of his life.

A DIVIDED EUROPE

When Drake was born, England was going through a very troubled period. Henry VIII was king (he reigned from 1509 until 1547). His first wife was the Spanish Catherine of Aragon. They had one child (the future queen, Mary I), but five other babies died. In his desperation to have a son, Henry divorced Catherine against the wishes of the **pope.** This set in motion events that led to England separating from the Roman **Catholic** Church and taking up Protestantism as its official religion. Europe itself was at war over religion, with Spain and the **Holy Roman Empire** as the main upholders of Catholicism. England was now Protestant, and countries like the **Low Countries,** the German States, and France were in the dreadful turmoil of **civil war.** Due to this backdrop, Drake came to dislike Catholicism and the Spanish.

Learning from an Uncle

Francis Drake had a rich uncle in Plymouth. John Hawkins was a merchant and **pirate** who owned ships that he sent out to trade with, and occasionally to rob, Spanish ships. He was also involved with the **slave trade,** stealing people from their villages on the west coast of Africa and selling them to rich Spaniards in Central and South America. He was very important in Drake's life, as well as a key figure in England's development as a powerful sea-going nation.

This is a portrait of John Hawkins, Drake's uncle, with whom Drake lived for many years. Hawkins was the first known Englishman to become involved with the slave trade.

Joining the Hawkins household

It was a custom of the time for parents to send their children to live with well-off relatives. Drake was brought up in the Hawkins household and may have received more education while there. When he was about eighteen, he was sent on a trading voyage to northeast Spain on one of Hawkins's ships—the *Tiger.* He held the position of purser on board the ship, which meant he was responsible for money matters, paying the crew and keeping records of the trading that was done. This was an important break for such a young man.

Learning his trade

Around the same time, Drake would have started to learn the skills needed for ocean voyaging. He would have gained knowledge of tides and currents, shoals (shallow areas), wind direction, and speed. He would have also learned how to use the ship's compass and other instruments for **navigation,** how to steer by the Sun and stars, and he would have developed the skills of **sounding the depth** and using judgment to decide where to find a harbor on foreign coasts.

This astrolabe is from the 16th century. These highly technical and very beautiful instruments were used by sailors as an aid for navigation at sea.

Drake would have built on the knowledge he had from sailing around Kent and France. However, in this new world of ocean travel, ships were out of sight of land for days, weeks, and even months on end. With nothing to steer by, sailors had to keep accurate information on the speed the ship was traveling and its direction to have any hope of knowing where they were. Drake would have also seen how captains dealt with the ordinary seamen. Discipline and fairness were vital for keeping a ship in order and the crew's spirits high. Voyages were always very dangerous. Storms, shipwrecks, disease, attack from other ships, as well as food and water running low, were all common events at sea. **Profits** were high on these trading and pirating adventures, but so were the risks.

A Seafaring Nation

This 19th-century statue of Sir Francis Drake is in Plymouth, England, a town whose destiny has been closely linked to the sea and the men who have sailed across it.

England is part of an island. Life at sea has been natural and inevitable for many of its inhabitants. In Drake's day, fishing was an important source of food and money, and ports all around the coastline harbored boats of various sizes. Any trade with foreign countries was done by sea—ships left England for France, the **Low Countries,** Spain, and further afield to Africa, India, the Caribbean, and South America. Drake would have seen ships of all kinds coming into port at Plymouth, where he lived with the Hawkins family. The local economy revolved around fishing and trade with France and Spain for goods like wine.

The growing importance of ships

The world was opening up to those, like Drake, who were experienced sailors and brave enough to risk long sea voyages. But such men needed ships that could withstand the ravages of storms. Drake's lifetime saw England becoming an important nation in Europe—a rival to the richest and most powerful country, Spain. For a while, England led the way in the development of the warship, which would become the main weapon of domination.

Drake and his uncle, John Hawkins, would later be heavily involved in both exploration and in the construction of a navy of ships able to challenge any power on Earth. Ships were the main means of making wealth from other lands—and that wealth could then be protected or increased using ships of war.

Protestantism

Elizabeth I established the **Protestant** Church in England in 1559, sending shock waves throughout Europe. Her father, Henry VIII, had already made himself "the supreme head on earth of the English Church" in direct defiance of the **pope.** Elizabeth inherited this role and strengthened the Protestant cause.

*This portrait of Queen Elizabeth I was painted in 1588 as part of the celebrations for England's victory over the **Spanish Armada.***

Drake's father, Edmund, was a Protestant vicar, and Drake took up the faith, linking it to the growing English **nationalism.** Philip II had become King of Spain in 1556. He wanted to unite all of Europe under the **Catholic** faith, so England was a natural enemy. Spain had taken over parts of South America and the Caribbean earlier in the 16th century. The wealth of gold, silver, and jewels taken from these lands helped build and keep the best army in Europe. English **pirates** started to raid ships bound for Spain carrying **New-World** treasure. Elizabeth increasingly turned a blind eye to these events, despite the complaints of Philip II to her government. England and Spain were on a collision course, both over their religions and over treasure and piracy.

Brave New World

Drake came into the world at an exciting time in terms of exploration by sea. In 1492, Christopher Columbus had sailed west to look for a sea route to lead Spain to the riches of India, avoiding the long and dangerous land trek. After a difficult 69-day journey across the Atlantic Ocean, he sighted land. His 3 ships and 90 men landed on an island in what is today the Bahamas, some 400 miles (650 kilometers) southeast of Florida. They moved on to other islands, including Cuba and Hispaniola. Columbus thought he had reached India, and called the native peoples "Indians." In fact, he had not found a new route to Asia, but had discovered a whole new continent for his adopted country of Spain—the Americas, or **New World.** He made three more voyages to Central America and the West Indies, but to the day he died he never realized he had discovered a new continental landmass.

A sea route to India

In 1497, the Portuguese Vasco da Gama became the first European to sail completely around Africa and enter the Indian Ocean.

The map shows the voyages of Christopher Columbus, Vasco da Gama, Amerigo Vespucci, and Ferdinand Magellan, all of whom helped change the course of European history.

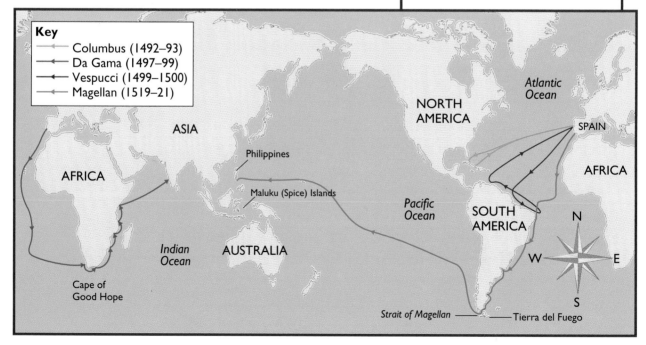

Key
— Columbus (1492–93)
— Da Gama (1497–99)
— Vespucci (1499–1500)
— Magellan (1519–21)

Atlantic Ocean
NORTH AMERICA
SPAIN
ASIA
AFRICA
Philippines
Maluku (Spice) Islands
Pacific Ocean
SOUTH AMERICA
AFRICA
N
Indian Ocean
AUSTRALIA
W — E
Cape of Good Hope
S
Strait of Magellan — Tierra del Fuego

He had discovered a sea route to the riches of the East, but it was a long voyage. Two years later, sailing the other way, Amerigo Vespucci discovered South America. In 1519, the Portuguese sailor Ferdinand Magellan set sail on the voyage that would first circumnavigate (travel all the way around) the globe. He went west around the southern tip of South America and eventually burst out into the Pacific Ocean. He did not survive the journey, but some of his crew made it back to Europe in 1522 with tales of wonder and great suffering.

MAPS AND SECRETS

Along with the growing skills of shipbuilding and **navigation,** the art of mapmaking helped change the world in which Drake lived. Maps had been around for hundreds of years. They usually represented the earth as flat (most people believed it was), and showed the very incomplete known world of the time. But the gaps were slowly being filled in by the ocean-going explorers. Magellan's expedition of 1519–22 had shown the world to be round and had opened up many new lands for the cartographers (map and globe makers) to tackle.

The development of printing had made mapmaking easier, but maps were still very inaccurate and always behind the times. For example, the sea trade route to India, discovered in 1497, was still not shown on some maps sold in 1570! One reason for this was secrecy. Governments did not want information easily available to rival countries, so discoveries were kept hidden. Drake's own **log** from his around-the-world voyage (1577–80) was hidden by Elizabeth's government for ten years after his return.

TYPVS ORBIS TERRARVM

QVID EI POTEST VIDERI MAGNVM IN REBVS HVMANIS, CVI AETERNITAS OMNIS, TOTIVSQVE MVNDI NOTA SIT MAGNITVDO. CICERO;

This engraved map of the world is from 1570.

Life on Board a Ship

Most ocean-going ships of the 16th century were fairly small. The ships used by Christopher Columbus were only about 70 feet (21 meters) long and 20 feet (6.5 meters) wide. With a crew of about 30 men, they sailed across thousands of miles of open sea and were away for months, even years, on end. When Francis Drake first took to the seas, there had been little improvement in the design of ships. Conditions on board were still cramped. The men slept where they could—on deck in the open or among the supplies below deck. The ships were made of wood and all leaked. Pumping out water was a major job.

A dangerous life

Sailors faced great danger on long voyages. Storms could drive ships off course and into unknown waters. If close to land, ships could be driven onto rocks. In very rough seas, they could be sunk by huge waves, or men could be swept overboard. Disease was a continual fear. Scurvy, a disease caused by lack of fresh vegetables and fruit, was common on long voyages. Fever was especially feared because it spread quickly—it could infect many of the crew at once, leaving the ship undermanned. On many of Drake's voyages to the Caribbean, illness was mentioned in the **log.**

A day in the life of a sailor

Drake and the other sailors would begin their day with prayers.

Ocean-going ships from the age of Drake looked like this. These were small and very cramped, and life on board was uncomfortable on long voyages.

This gathering was important for **morale,** as it helped the men remember the world they had left behind, that of their country and their God. The crew was divided into groups called watches. A watch was usually on duty for four hours, then rested for four hours while another watch was on duty. This happened 24 hours a day, every day. There were always jobs to be done. The ship needed tending, sails mending, water pumping, and food cooking. During a storm, all able-bodied men had to help keep the ship afloat and on course. If a storm went on for days, this could be exhausting.

Every sailor dreaded storms and shoals—shallow areas where rock might lurk under the water's surface. Both spelled one thing—shipwreck!

Discipline

Mutiny was every captain's worry. To avoid this, discipline on board was very harsh. Men were flogged for small failings, like falling asleep on watch. Continual disobedience was punished by death. On his around-the-world voyage at the end of the 1570s, Drake executed one of his crew because he threatened Drake's control over his men.

In sailors' words:

"We ate only old biscuit reduced to powder, all full of worms and stinking of the urine that the rats made on it. And we drank water that was yellow and stinking."

(Antonio Pigafetta, a sailor on Magellan's voyage early in the 1520s, describing life after four months at sea)

"It rotted all my gums, which gave out a black and putrid blood. My thighs and lower legs were black, and I was forced to use my knife each day to cut into the flesh, to release this black and foul blood."

(A 15th-century sailor describing symptoms of scurvy)

Robbing Spanish Galleons

Between the 1560s and early 1570s, Francis Drake learned his trade as a seaman working for John Hawkins, traveling to the Caribbean to rob Spanish ships full of treasure. Hawkins was probably the first Englishman to be involved in the **slave trade.** He was a rich man and not fussy about how he made his money. French **pirates** had started the trend of robbing Spanish ships in the 1520s. Englishmen like Hawkins were quick to catch on. The Spanish **colonies** in Central and South America were producing lots of silver and gold. Large ships called **galleons** were sent out to bring this treasure home to Spain. Pirates could become rich very quickly if they had a lucky strike. It was for this gamble that they risked their lives—they were hanged if caught.

SPANISH TREASURE

In 1545, the Spanish found silver at a place called Potosi in modern-day Bolivia. Three years later they discovered more silver in Mexico. These mines, combined with the gold mines of the Incas and Aztecs, made Spain the richest and most powerful country in Europe. They sent two fleets of ships a year to take out food, clothing, wine, oil, and equipment to their colonies and to bring the treasure home. It was these ships that the French and English pirates targeted.

This 16th-century engraving shows a Spanish treasure ship being plundered by Sir Francis Drake and his men.

Caca Fogo.

Caca Plata.

Buccaneer or pirate?

Francis Drake probably started his career as a pirate. However, he ended his life as a rich man and a member of the Elizabethan ruling classes, having been mayor of Plymouth, a **member of Parliament,** a trusted adviser to the queen on naval matters, and the hero of the defeat of the **Spanish Armada.** It seems that at some point in his career he moved from being an outlaw, or pirate, to being a **buccaneer.** A buccaneer may have behaved like a pirate, but he worked with the approval of his king or queen—in Drake's case, Queen Elizabeth. Although the queen referred to him as "my little pirate," she actually admired what he was doing. Drake was therefore under her protection. When he returned from his voyages, he gave a large part of the gold and silver he had taken from the Spanish to the royal treasury. The queen in turn gave him "Letters of the Marque," which represented her protection.

King Philip II of Spain reigned from 1556 to 1598.

King Philip II of Spain was furious about this situation and complained to Elizabeth through his minister at her court in London. She played a game with the Spanish king, promising to stop Drake's actions, but never actually doing so.

Drake's Early Voyages

You can follow Drake's voyage in the *Tiger* on the map on pages 42–43.

We do not know exactly when Drake went on his first voyage for John Hawkins, but it was probably in the late 1550s, when he was in his late teens. He sailed in the *Tiger* across the Bay of Biscay to the northeast coast of Spain to trade. He may have also been involved in piracy at this early stage, as the *Tiger* was one of Hawkins's light raiding vessels.

Drake obviously made money, despite his youth. There are records showing he invested in goods for a trade visit to the coast of Africa only a few years later. English trading vessels were visiting the Guinea coast and bringing back gold, ivory, and the rare and valuable pepper. Hawkins and the young Drake wanted their share of this profitable trade. Hawkins made important trade connections on the Spanish Canary Islands at this time, using the port as a base for his voyages to the African coast. When he looked further afield for trade, to the Caribbean, he continued to use the Canaries as a place to take on board water and supplies for the long Atlantic voyage.

This is the west coast of Africa, where the young Drake may have made some of his early long-distance sea voyages.

The Spanish **colonies** in Central and South America wanted slaves to work in the mines and on the plantations. Portuguese and Spanish ships took people from their villages in Africa and sold them to these colonies. This practice was condemned by some European church leaders, but not by all. Some argued that these slaves were lucky, because they would be baptized and their souls saved. The fact remains that thousands upon thousands were forcibly taken to the New World, many dying on the journey due to overcrowded and dirty conditions, poor food, and disease.

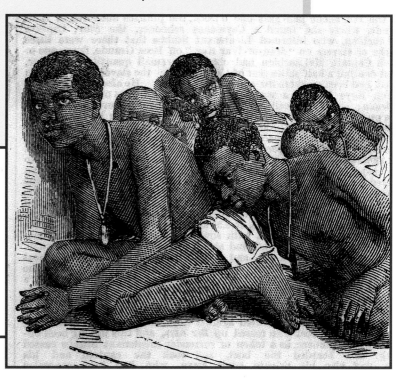

A 19th-century engraving shows the cramped conditions that slaves would have suffered in the hold of a ship. Many died on the voyage to the West Indies.

Hawkins and Drake in the West Indies

Hawkins was one of the first Englishmen to challenge the domination of the Spanish and Portuguese in Africa and the West Indies. Between 1562 and 1565 he led two voyages that captured hundreds of slaves in Africa and took them across the ocean to the **New World,** trading them for treasure and hides. He had very powerful backers for these ventures, including rich London merchants, government and naval officials, and royal **courtiers** such as the Earl of Leicester and the Earl of Pembroke. The queen herself lent one of her own ships, the 785-ton (712-tonne) *Jesus of Lubeck,* for Hawkins and Drake's second voyage. The Spanish king ordered his officials in the New World not to trade with the English, but his orders were largely ignored. The colonists in South America, Panama, and Mexico were only too pleased to receive trade and were not very fussy as to whether the ships were Spanish, Portuguese, English, or French.

"The Troublesome Voyage"

Francis Drake's father, Edmund, died on Boxing Day, December 26, 1566. Francis, his eldest son, was away in the West Indies. He heard the news when he returned in September 1567. However, he had little time to grieve. John Hawkins was planning the biggest slaving expedition to leave English shores. It would be a difficult voyage from start to finish. Hawkins wrote an account of it a couple of years later, calling it his "Troublesome Voyage."

Queen Elizabeth is pictured here on her throne, addressing an assembly of the Lords of the **Realm.**

Storms

Six ships of various sizes gathered in Plymouth in September 1567. Two of them, including the now aging *Jesus of Lubeck,* belonged to the queen. The financial backers and shareholders included merchants from the city of London, influential naval men, and **courtiers** and ministers of the court of Elizabeth. The ships set sail under the overall command of John Hawkins on October 2, 1567. There was a total of 408 men. Francis Drake may have started the voyage on board the *Jesus,* as one of the principal officers. Or he may have captained a much smaller vessel, the *Judith.* Either way, he had obviously earned the respect of Hawkins and other men and gained promotion. The queen herself gave him orders to sail to Guinea in Africa, take slaves, and sell them in the West Indies. The fleet carried English cloth with which to trade. However, only four days out from port, a storm struck the fleet. It lasted for days, and the *Judith* became separated from the other ships. The storm caused so much damage that Hawkins almost turned the expedition around and headed for home.

The Canaries and the Guinea coast

All the ships managed to come back together and struggled on to Tenerife in the Canary Islands. Here the fleet was to restock with supplies and fresh water. However, the Spanish on the island were unfriendly. Philip II of Spain had ordered that Hawkins and his **"pirates"** were not to be helped. Because Hawkins's fleet was so well armed, they eventually got what they wanted and continued on their way to the west coast of Africa.

This is the rocky coast of the Canary Islands. John Hawkins used these islands to take on board food and water before embarking on longer voyages across the Atlantic.

Taking slaves

The fleet spent weeks on the African coast, raiding inland villages to capture people to sell as slaves. In all they took around 500 to 600 people and packed them into the holds of their ships for the long voyage across the Atlantic Ocean. In the process, Hawkins lost about 60 men, mainly from skirmishes with local inhabitants. Many more of his crew were wounded.

You can follow Hawkins and Drake's voyage on the map on pages 42–43.

The Spanish Main

The voyage across the Atlantic lasted about two months. The ships were well supplied, so the men were still in reasonable health when they next saw land. Hawkins ate his meals with other important members of the crew of the *Jesus,* one of whom may have been Drake, using silver and fine linen at a table. Twice a day the men gathered for prayers. If a crew member showed signs of **Catholicism** he was disciplined.

Sighting land

The first land sighted was the island of Dominica. Here the ships took on board fresh water. They then sailed south towards the coast of South America and the **Spanish Main.** They stopped at the island of Margarita to trade their Devon cloth for meat and other provisions with the Spanish, before moving on to the mainland port of Borburata. Hawkins had traded here in the past. They arrived in April 1568 and stayed for around two months, trying to get a trading license from the governor. However, orders had been received from Spain that the colonies were not to trade with Hawkins. Despite his persistence, Hawkins was unable to sell his slaves for provisions and treasure.

*This map shows Spanish territories in the **New World,** including the Caribbean mainland coast of South America, known as the Spanish Main.*

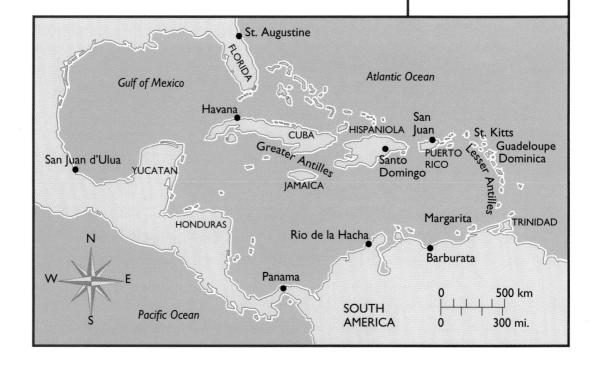

Drake in command

It is likely that Hawkins sent Drake with some of the ships to try trading further along the coast. Again, the hopes of the English were dashed. Hawkins also sent Drake to inspect one of their main destinations, Rio de la Hacha. But when his ships came into sight of the port, Spanish cannons opened fire on them. However, when Hawkins arrived with the rest of the fleet, he sent ashore 200 armed men to take the town and force the governor to trade with them. This worked, and they were able to sell about 200 black slaves to the local plantation owners.

Failure and return

The fleet was again caught by a storm while sailing north. It lasted for about four days, at the end of which the ships were again split up. One vessel, the *William and John,* never found the rest again and had to make its own way back to England. The remaining fleet gathered off the coast of Florida. It headed for a port called San Juan d'Ulua, in present-day Mexico, to make repairs and try to trade. But they were tricked by the **viceroy** of New Spain (as the area was called) and, after a brief battle, they had to make out to sea. Drake, in the *Judith,* became separated and made his own way back to Plymouth. One hundred sailors were abandoned on the Mexican coast, and few of these saw their homes again. The voyage was an economic failure and a blow to England's prestige. Drake was never to forget the treachery of the Spanish viceroy. He was to quickly become master of his own voyages and planned not only to get richer, but also to get even with the Spanish.

¶ A true declaration of the *troublesome voy-* adge of M. John Hau- kins to the parties of Guynea and the west Indies, in the yea- res of our Lord 1567. and 1568.

¶ Imprinted at Londō in Poules Church- yarde, by Thomas Purfo- te for Lucas Harrison, dwelling at the sig- ne of the Crane.

Anno. 1569.

This is the front cover of John Hawkins's account of the disastrous expedition of 1567–68. He called it the "Troublesome Voyage."

Wealth and Marriage

Just where and when Francis Drake met his first wife, Mary Newman, we do not know. The records do not even clearly tell us where she came from. She may have come from Devon's neighboring county of Cornwall, but a cousin of Drake's wrote that he thought she came from London. However, we do know that Drake and Mary Newman were married at St. Budeaux church near Plymouth on July 4, 1569. They were together for just over thirteen years but had no children. Mary probably saw little of her husband, as he was at sea most of the time, making his reputation in the West Indies and on the **Spanish Main.** Mary died young, but lived long enough to benefit from the considerable wealth that Drake made plundering Spanish ships.

St. Budeaux church, near Plymouth, is where Drake married Mary Newman in July 1569.

Drake in the West Indies

Drake had made enough money on his early voyages to take a wife and also finance his own voyages to the West Indies. He took to the seas again in late 1569, using Devon woolen cloth to trade with, taking slaves on board in Guinea, and then transporting them to the West Indies. This set the pattern for further trips, in 1571 and 1572, all lasting about a year.

Drake and his men encountered many hardships, including disease, storms, and skirmishes with the Spanish, but on the whole were very successful. When Drake returned home in the summer of 1573, he was fantastically wealthy and known and feared by the Spanish and all in the West Indies. He had also become a favorite of his queen, mostly because he gave so much of his gold and silver taken from Spanish ships to the English **treasury.**

Francis Drake bought property in and around Plymouth. He had servants, fine clothes, and was known at the court of the queen. However, many people thought of him as a mere **pirate** and would have nothing to do with him.

*This is part of the coastline of present-day Colombia, in South America. This was a landscape that Drake would get to know very well on his voyages in the **New World**.*

UPPING THE STAKES

The Spanish were learning that if they wanted to protect their treasure ships, they needed to build ships that could travel with the convoys and keep the pirates and **buccaneers** away, and they also needed to fortify key towns on the Main, Panama, and Mexican coasts. They did so from about 1568 onwards. In response to this, Drake and other pirates developed small boats, called **pinnaces,** that could be rowed close to shore or other boats. They used these to outmaneuver the larger Spanish ships, while still being able to get their hands on the treasure ships.

Drake was now his own master, though he was not well educated and seemed ill-mannered to some people at court, where he was regarded as "a private man of mean quality." In 1575, he was involved in a military campaign in Ireland with the queen's favorite **courtier,** the Earl of Essex. Although it was unsuccessful, Drake's role in it brought him recognition. He also got involved with Hawkins in importing produce from Zante, one of the Greek Ionian islands. Drake was constantly looking for new opportunities.

Robert Devereux, Earl of Essex (1567–1601), became the queen's favorite in 1585, but fell from grace and was executed in 1601 for high treason.

A secret plan

Drake's biggest undertaking was hatched in secrecy by the queen and some of her ministers. He was to sail down the coast of South America and around the feared Cape Horn, through the Strait of Magellan. No English ship had yet made this journey. He was to take his fleet into the Pacific Ocean and explore the coastline. He was also to raid as many Spanish ships and ports in the **New World** as possible, taking treasure where he could. The true mission of the fleet was hidden. Letters were sent between ministers suggesting Drake was off to the Mediterranean and the North African coast. This pretense was kept up, even with the sailors themselves, until the fleet reached South America.

Preparing to set sail

The queen lent her ship, the *Swallow,* and Drake used his own vessel, the *Pelican.* Other ships in the fleet were the *Elizabeth* and the *Marigold,* a small supply ship called the *Swan,* and a **pinnace,** the *Benedict.* All were well-armed vessels. The total crew numbered about 170. They set sail from Plymouth in November 1577. However, a storm off the coast of Cornwall led to damage and the entire fleet returned to harbor. After some repairs, they set off again in mid-December.

A storm at sea was a major hazard for small wooden sailing ships of the 16th century.

Sailing Around the World

The fleet went first to North Africa, and then down the coast. Drake sailed on to the Cape Verde islands, where he captured a large Portuguese merchant ship. The captain, Nuno de Silva, knew the coast of South America well, so Drake kept him for the rest of the voyage. The ships headed west across the Atlantic on February 2, 1578 and took over two months to make the crossing. They had calm seas for three weeks, but water and food were running low. Tempers among the men were short, and Drake fell out with one of his captains, Thomas Doughty (see box).

TRIAL AND EXECUTION

Thomas Doughty was eventually tried for **mutiny**. Various members of the crew spoke out against him. He was found guilty and beheaded on July 2, 1578 at Port San Julian, off the coast of present-day Argentina.

The Strait of Magellan

Storms had reduced the fleet to three ships—Drake's *Pelican,* the *Marigold,* and the *Elizabeth.* At the Strait of Magellan, strong winds and vicious seas raged most of the time. They spent all September edging past Tierra del Fuego, but then the *Marigold* was lost in a storm. The *Elizabeth* and the *Pelican,* with Drake on board, were separated in a further storm. At the end of October, the *Pelican* (which Drake had renamed the *Golden Hind*) headed north on its own, up the Pacific coast of South America.

Drake had to pass through the Strait of Magellan to go from the Atlantic to the Pacific Ocean.

Claiming California for the queen

After many adventures navigating the coast of South America, Drake and his men landed on new territory—what we know of today as California. Here they met native peoples, who treated them with honor. Before Drake left, he claimed the land for his queen and country.

Finishing the voyage

Leaving "Nova Albion" (New England) behind, Drake struck out across the ocean, heading west into the unknown. After more hardships, they struck land around the Philippines and went on to the Spice Islands. Passing close to the north coast of Australia (but without seeing it or knowing that it was there), the *Golden Hind* entered the Indian Ocean. Eventually they sailed around the tip of Africa and up into more familiar waters. Drake and his men arrived home in the autumn of 1580. The voyage was the longest ever undertaken, in both time and distance. Magellan's voyage in the early 1520s had been the first to go around the world; Drake's was the second. Drake had much treasure to delight the queen. In April 1581, she knighted him on board his ship, the *Golden Hind,* which she ordered to be kept as a monument to this heroic journey.

YOU CAN FOLLOW DRAKE'S VOYAGE ON THE *GOLDEN HIND* ON THE MAP ON PAGES 42–43.

This 19th-century engraving shows Drake being knighted by Queen Elizabeth on board his own ship, the Golden Hind, *on his return from his around-the-world voyage.*

A National Hero

Drake was now a national hero. Poems were written about his exploits. He was also very rich and owned several estates, including Buckland Abbey in Devon. He was making the shift from being a rough man of the sea, a **pirate** and merchant adventurer, to being a renowned figure in court and country, and a knight of the **realm.** He was rubbing shoulders with great **courtiers** and ministers of the queen's **Privy Council.** He was soon to become involved in national security and the defense of the realm against the old enemy: the Spanish and their detested **Catholic** faith. He was elected **Lord Mayor** of Plymouth in September 1581, and in the same year became a **member of Parliament.** However, he always remained at heart a plain, ill-educated sailor who spoke his mind. This endeared him to the ordinary people, but most of the ministers only put up with him because he brought vast fortunes to the national **treasury.**

> *"Both Turk and Pope and all our foes Do dread this Drake where'er he goes."*
>
> (From a popular poem written about Drake in 1587)

Buckland Abbey, in Devon, was one of several estates that Drake bought with the huge wealth he acquired.

Death of a wife and remarriage

Drake's first wife, Mary, was probably from an ordinary background, but she had become Lady Drake when her husband was knighted by Queen Elizabeth I. The **parish register** of St. Andrews in Plymouth names "*The Lady Marie the wiffe of Sir Frauncis Drake knight*" as having been buried there on January 25, 1583. We do not know how she died, nor do we have any record of Drake's grief.

Drake remarried in February 1585. His bride was young, beautiful, and the daughter of a rich nobleman, Sir George Sydenham. Her name was Elizabeth. She was brought up at Combe Sydenham, a large house and estate in Somerset. She was well educated and a member of privileged society. Marriage to Elizabeth sums up how far Drake had traveled from his roots as a poor boy from Tavistock learning the ways of the sea.

The beautiful and aristocratic Elizabeth Sydenham was Drake's second wife.

"Singeing the King of Spain's Beard"

Life in the 1580s was not all to do with domestic affairs, politics, and wealth. Drake remained a man of the sea at heart. He also craved adventure and became restless on land. One notable exploit was destroying 24 Spanish ships and provisions, meant for an invasion of England, in their own harbor of Cadiz in southwest Spain. Drake had sailed with a fleet, including four of the queen's war ships, in early April 1587. They captured many Spanish and Portuguese merchant vessels before sailing right into the heart of Cadiz and wrecking the Spanish fleet. They called this triumph "singeing the King of Spain's beard"!

31

War on the Horizon

When Drake raided Cadiz and destroyed so many ships, he set back Spanish plans for an invasion of England. However, open war between the two countries was inevitable. Drake played his own part in bringing this about. He had raided many treasure ships and ports of the Spanish, in home water and in the **New World.** He had embraced England's new **Protestant** religion, and used it as an important reason to fight the **Catholic** Spanish. He was not alone in this—many powerful countrymen felt the same way and wanted war with Spain. For their part, the Spanish felt that England was a thorn in the side of the **Holy Roman Empire.** For example, England had sent an army led by the Earl of Leicester to support Dutch Protestants rebelling against Spanish rule in their country. England needed to be brought to heel. An invasion was planned and, in spite of Drake, it was going to go ahead. King Philip II of Spain put all his resources behind making it happen.

The Spanish navy was formidable and had defeated the Turkish fleet at the Battle of Lepanto, near Greece, in 1571.

The Armada gathers

Early in 1588, King Philip II of Spain put one of his noblemen, the Duke of Medina Sidonia, in charge of his greatest fleet, the **Spanish Armada.** It was harbored at Lisbon in Portugal and consisted of around 30,000 men, 130 ships, 2,500 cannon, 124,000 cannon balls, 7,000 hand-guns, 6,000 grenades, 11,000 pikes, and 12 siege guns. The war **galleons** were large, difficult to move, and slow. This was important in the battles to follow.

Tactics

The Spanish crew consisted of sailors, who manned the ships, and soldiers, who would be involved in the fighting. These soldiers made up over half the invasion force. The Spanish plans were to move in alongside the English ships, blast them at close quarters with their cannon, then board the crippled ships with their soldiers. They would have a large army on the coast, ready to invade England once the Spanish navy had destroyed the English ships. These plans depended entirely on getting close enough to the English ships to board them and defeat their crews. However, the English commanders, who included Sir Francis Drake, had other ideas. Their ships were smaller, lighter, and quicker. They were to use these advantages in the coming engagements.

The Spanish Armada

After a false start, the Duke of Medina Sidonia and the **Spanish Armada** set sail on July 21, 1588. Within four days they reached English waters and sent word to the Spanish army in the **Low Countries** to prepare for invasion. Meanwhile, English spies under Sir Francis Walsingham passed on news about the Spanish movements. Beacons were lit across the south coast to warn people of the approach of the Armada. The English captains planned to fight the Spanish at sea and stop the army from setting foot on English soil.

The English navy

Both Francis Drake and John Hawkins had been involved with upgrading the ships of the English navy. There were 197 vessels ready for the coming battle—smaller and better armed than the Spanish. Most were old, but the newer **galleons** were better fighting ships than anything the Spanish had. In keeping with the English tactics for fighting at sea, there were only 16,000 men on board, all of them sailors rather than soldiers.

Conflict

There were five major confrontations in the English Channel in July and August of 1588. The first three of these did not produce many results. The English, led by Lord Howard, kept out of range of the Spanish cannon and were divided into four squadrons to pick off the Spanish galleons, but the Spanish held their formation. Eventually the Armada reached the French port of Calais, where they took on fresh water and food.

This is a painting of the decisive Battle of Gravelines. By the end of the day, the Spanish ships were in disorder and unable to reassemble.

Fireships and defeat

Howard now used a master stroke—unmanned ships were set on fire and directed at the anchored Spanish fleet. No damage was done, but the Armada was scattered in the Channel. Some managed to regroup in time for the decisive Battle of Gravelines (named after a place in France). The two fleets fought for nine hours, the English firing their cannon shot more quickly and accurately into the Spanish, but keeping far enough away so that the Spanish soldiers could not board them. Around 1,000 Spaniards were killed and many wounded.

The Armada was now on the run. Strong winds drove the ships north as far as Scotland. Over the coming weeks, storms did more damage to the Spanish than the might of the English navy had. Only 60 ships and half the total number of crew and soldiers made it back to Spain. The rest were drowned or killed, mainly off the coast of Ireland. Those that survived struggled back to Spain in late September. England was saved from invasion, and the Spanish army in the Low Countries withdrew.

THE ENGLISH COMMANDERS

In overall command of the fleet was Lord Howard in his ship the *Ark Royal*. Drake was vice admiral (second in command) of the fleet, and sailed in the *Revenge*. The largest ship in the fleet, the *Triumph*, was captained by the famous explorer Martin Frobisher. Drake's uncle, John Hawkins, was also a captain in the fleet.

With the Armada defeated, Elizabeth's ministers decided to attack while Spain and Portugal's defenses were weak. The plan needed to be carried out quickly, but delays occurred, allowing the Spanish to build up their forces. Drake went to London to discuss plans with the **Privy Council.** He was given joint charge of the expedition with a man named John Norris. Norris would be in command of land forces, and Drake would captain the fleet.

Conflicting plans

The queen wanted the expedition to find and destroy all Armada ships that had struggled back to northern Spain, and to take the

islands of the Azores so they could capture Spanish treasure ships sailing past on their way to Spain. However, Dom Antonio de Crato, a Portuguese nobleman living in London, was willing to pay for help to claim the throne of Portugal, which had come under Spanish rule. Ever impressed by the thought of riches, Drake made plans with Norris to invade Lisbon, the capital of Portugal, and place Dom Antonio on the throne. The forces gathered to achieve these aims were huge—a land army of 19,000 men and around 100 ships to transport them.

Sir Francis Drake is pictured here in the 1580s, a wealthy man in fine clothes with his own coat of arms. His hand spans the globe on which it rests, indicating his success in sailing completely around the world.

A doomed adventure

They sailed on April 18, 1589, heading for La Coruña on the northwest coast of Spain. They expected to find hundreds of Spanish ships, but the port was empty. The town was taken by Norris's men, but they could not take the well-defended upper section because they lacked expensive heavy siege-guns. After two weeks they retreated, having achieved little.

They sailed on to take Peniche, a town in Portugal, and the capital, Lisbon, but the campaign was a disaster. Drake showed no ability in conducting a siege of heavily fortified and well-defended towns. Both Norris's army and Drake's fleet suffered serious losses. In the end they were forced to withdraw. Norris returned to England, and Drake made for the Azores to try to capture treasure. The whole episode was a personal disaster for Drake. He had not carried out the queen's aims of finding and destroying Spanish warships. Instead he had sailed on to Lisbon and even there had failed. This perhaps suggests Drake remained a **pirate** at heart. He was motivated by short-term personal gain (wealth), not by tactical military advantages. He also showed he was not a military commander and could not handle a big campaign to capture a major city. He was more at home on the high seas, taking treasure ships or laying siege to small Spanish colonial towns.

Drake sailed past the coast of Portugal on his disastrous attempt to capture Lisbon and put Dom Antonio on the throne.

The Final Voyage

Although the great Armada of 1588 had failed, the Spanish continued to plan invasion. In the 1590s, smaller fleets attacked the west coast of England, on one occasion burning the port of Penzance. The queen turned to Drake and Hawkins. There were rumors that the Spanish planned to invade Ireland and then send a fleet to invade England. Drake and Hawkins were ordered to get their ships together and seek out and destroy this fleet, if it existed. The two old **pirates** also had plans of their own—to raid Panama.

YOU CAN FIND THE SITE OF DRAKE'S FINAL BATTLE ON THE MAP ON PAGE 22.

Trouble in the Canaries

Drake and Hawkins were given joint command of the expedition, which caused some decision-making problems. They would have 27 ships in all, divided into 2 squadrons. Both men were getting on in years. Drake was in his 50s and slower than he had been.

They left Plymouth on August 28, 1595, sailing for the Canary Islands—a common stopping point for ships running out of food supplies. When they tried to land, however, the Spanish resisted, and four men were killed in a skirmish. Some of the English crew were taken prisoner and gave away all details of the fleet's plans to sail to Panama. The Spanish sent a fast ship to the West Indies to warn their fleet and ports. Drake had lost the element of surprise.

This is the fortified island of Puerto Rico, where Drake came under heavy fire on his last voyage in 1595.

Panama and fever

The fleet sailed on to the West Indies, reaching the Lesser Antilles by October 26. They spent ten days preparing their ships for battle and taking on water and food. John Hawkins fell ill and died on November 11. Things were destined to get worse. Anchored off Puerto Rico, the fleet came under heavy fire from the port. Drake was eating at the time and narrowly escaped death. When they finally arrived off the coast of Panama, a thousand men were sent inland with a man called Baskerville in charge, with the aim of capturing the city. Drake was to sail up river with reinforcements. However, it was the rainy season, and the marching men were delayed by mud on the hillsides. After a brief battle with the Spanish, they retreated to the ships. It was another failure for Drake.

The fleet turned away from Panama and stopped at a small island called Escudo to rest and refit the ships. Fever swept through the crew. Drake himself fell ill and, after a few days, died of dysentery, a stomach disease, on January 28, 1596.

In the disease-infested jungle and rivers of Panama in Central America, Drake caught dysentery and died in January 1596.

In a crew member's words:

"Since our return from Panama he [Drake] never carried mirth nor joy in his face."

Buried at sea

"His [Drake's] corpse being laid into a coffin of lead . . . the Trumpets in doleful manner echoing out this lamentation for so great a loss, and all the Cannons in the fleet were discharged according to the custom of all Sea Funeral obsequies [ceremonies]."

(A crew member)

The Legacy of a Pirate

Adored by his countrymen and feared and loathed by the Spanish, Drake passed quickly into the realm of literature and legend. At the news of Drake's death, the poet Charles FitzGeffrey wrote an epic poem about him. All England mourned for him, while the Spanish and other **Catholics** rejoiced. For them, it was as if the devil himself had been defeated.

In the king's words

When the aging and sick King Philip II of Spain heard of Drake's death, he is reported to have said,

"It is good news and now I will get well."

Drake and the English navy

Drake had shown that for a nation to be truly great, it needed a powerful and flexible navy. He was only the second man, and the first Englishman, to sail around the world. He advised on the development of new ships and helped build up England's defenses around the coast, including at Plymouth. Ships at this time provided the key to movement around the globe. Whoever had the strongest navy would rule the seas. Ships were also the key to developing **colonies** and eventually empires in foreign lands.

In this respect, Drake's raids on treasure ships and exploration were very important. Sailors continued in these raids after his death, and on a national level, England's navy was vital to the growth of its power and influence abroad over the coming years.

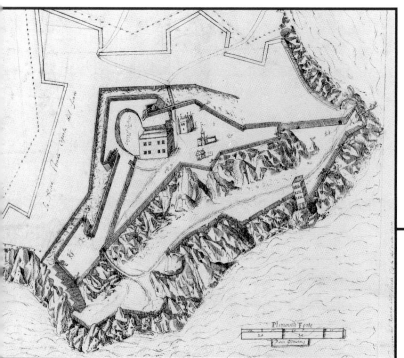

Plans were drawn up to build and develop the defenses of key English ports, such as Plymouth. Drake was active in helping advise on matters like these.

Drake and the patriots

Drake has left another legacy for the English. He is seen as one of the heroes who, at the birth of what is modern England, had a profound effect on its course in history. When times have been dark for England, Drake has been recalled, like Robin Hood, Richard the Lionheart, and King Arthur. A good example is a poem Henry Newbolt wrote about Drake in 1895, when conflict with Germany looked possible. His lines are designed to bring out the **patriotism** of Drake:

> *"Take my drum to
> England, hang it by the shore;
> Strike it when your powder's running low.
> If the Dons sight Devon, I'll quit the port of Heaven,
> And drum them up the Channel as we drummed
> them long ago."*

The "Dons" are meant to be the Spanish, but they could represent any enemy of England.

Drake was quoted at the outset of the Second World War. He was even quoted by the British Prime Minister Margaret Thatcher in the 1980s! Drake, the self-made Englishman, **pirate,** and knight of the **realm,** practical and daring, but also self-interested and ruthless, has become a symbol for England that can be summoned, as the poem says, by striking the legendary drum.

This drum is said to have been owned by Drake. Nearly 400 years after Drake's death, the poet Henry Newbolt drew on the idea of Drake being able to return to help the nation in times of trouble, summoned by the beating of this drum.

Map of Drake's Voyages

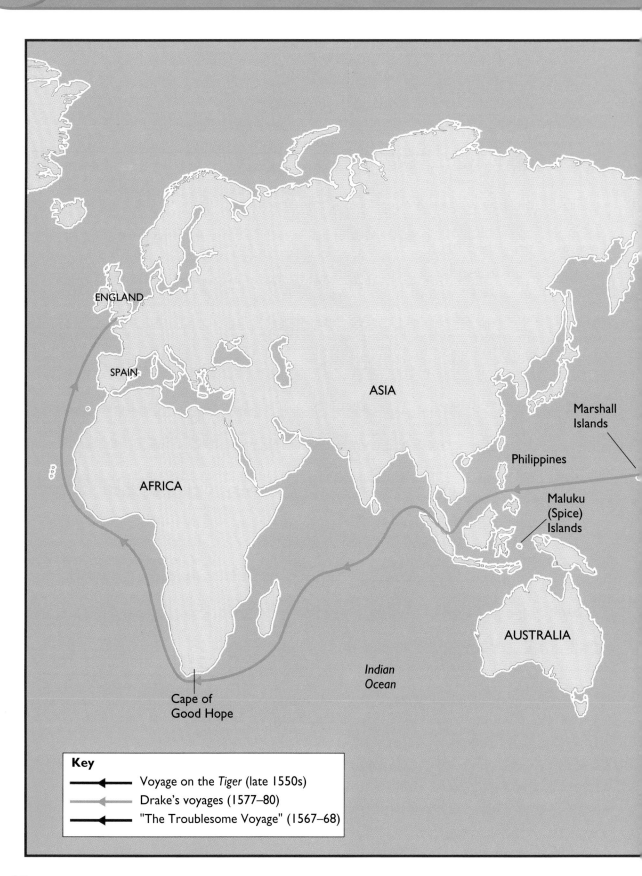

ENGLAND

SPAIN

AFRICA

ASIA

Marshall
Islands

Philippines

Maluku
(Spice)
Islands

AUSTRALIA

Indian
Ocean

Cape of
Good Hope

Key

⟵ Voyage on the *Tiger* (late 1550s)

⟵ Drake's voyages (1577–80)

⟵ "The Troublesome Voyage" (1567–68)

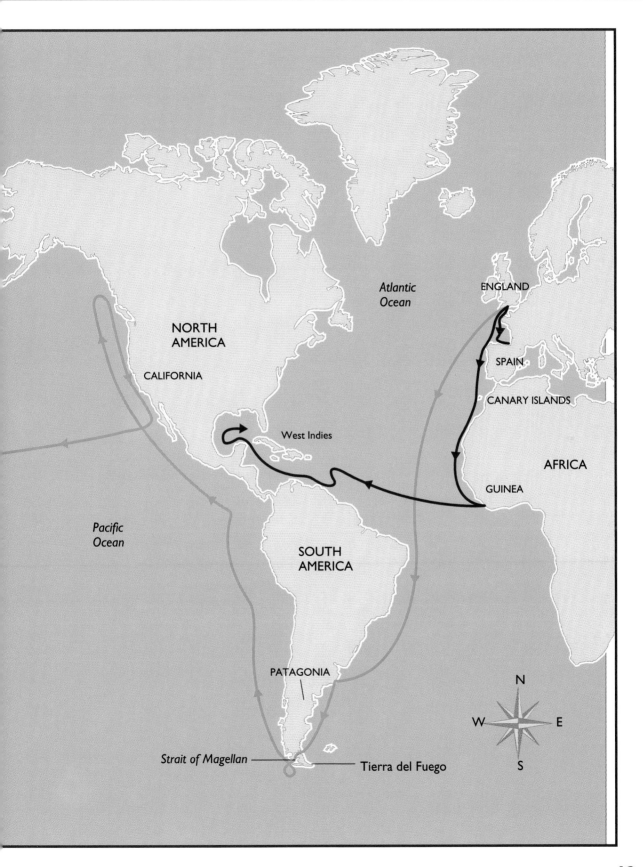

NORTH
AMERICA

CALIFORNIA

Atlantic
Ocean

ENGLAND

SPAIN

CANARY ISLANDS

AFRICA

GUINEA

West Indies

Pacific
Ocean

SOUTH
AMERICA

PATAGONIA

N

W   E

S

Strait of Magellan ————— Tierra del Fuego

Timeline

1519 The Portuguese explorer Ferdinand Magellan sets sail on the voyage that will become the first to circumnavigate the globe.

1540 (?) Francis Drake is born near Tavistock in Devon.

1558 Elizabeth I becomes Queen of England.

Around this time, Drake first goes to sea with his uncle, John Hawkins.

1560–70 Drake spends much of his time at sea in the Caribbean, carrying goods and slaves to trade with the Spanish, but also plundering Spanish treasure ships.

1564 William Shakespeare is born.

1566 Drake's father, Edmund, dies on Boxing Day, December 26.

1569 Drake marries Mary Newman on July 4.

1577 Drake sets sail on the voyage that will take him around the world.

1578 Drake passes through the Strait of Magellan and sails into the Pacific Ocean.

1579 Drake lands in California and claims it for the English crown.

1580 Drake and his men arrive back in England on November 3, having sailed around the world.

1581 Drake is knighted by Elizabeth I.

1583 Drake's wife, Mary Newman, dies.

1585 Drake marries Elizabeth Sydenham in February, and raids Spanish ports and treasure ships in the Caribbean.

1586 The Spanish draw up plans to invade England.

1587 Drake attacks Cadiz, an important Spanish port, in April.

1588 Medina Sidonia is chosen to take charge of the Spanish Armada.

July 21	Armada sets sail for England.
July 29	Drake and the English fleet set sail from Plymouth harbor.
July 31–August 4	The Battles of Plymouth, Portland, and the Isle of Wight are fought.
August 6	Spanish Armada shelters in French port of Calais.
August 7 and 8	English use burning ships to disperse Spanish fleet.
August 8	The decisive Battle of Gravelines is fought.
August 31	The Spanish officially abandon the invasion.
September	Many Spanish ships are lost in storms around the Scottish and Irish coasts.

1589	Drake leads a fleet to Spain and Portugal, ending in disaster.
1595	Drake sets sail for Canary Islands on August 28.
	John Hawkins, Drake's uncle, dies on November 11.
1596	Drake dies of dysentery in the Caribbean on January 28.
1603	Elizabeth I dies.
1604	The Spanish and English sign a peace treaty in London.

More Books to Read

Bard, Roberta. *Francis Drake: First Englishman to Circle the Globe*. Danbury, Conn.: Children's Press, 1992.

Barron's Educational Editors. *Drake and 16th-Century Explorers*. Hauppauge, N.Y.: Barron's Educational Series, 1998.

Grolier Educational Corporation. *The Grolier Student Library of Explorers and Exploration*. Bethel, Conn.: Grolier Educational, 1998.

Marrin, Albert. *The Sea King: Sir Francis Drake and His Times*. New York: Simon & Schuster Children's, 1995.

Smith, Alice. Edited by William H. Goetzmann. Introduction by Michael Collins. *Sir Francis Drake and the Struggle for an Ocean Empire*. Broomall, Pa.: Chelsea House Publishers, 1993.

Glossary

ambassador   person who represents his or her king, queen, or government at the court of another king or queen

buccaneer   someone who behaved like a pirate, but had the backing of a monarch

Catholic   usually applied to a person who is a member of the Roman Catholic Church, led by the pope in Rome

Catholicism   faith and practice of Catholic Christianity

civil war   war between groups of people living in the same country

colony   area of land in another country that people take over and settle in

courtier   person at the court of a king or a queen

dissolved   brought to an end, broken up, and/or stripped of all rights

galleon   large sailing ship of the 15th to the 18th centuries used for transporting treasure from the New World or as a warship

Holy Roman Empire   Christian revival of the ancient Roman Empire—started in the Middle Ages and made up of much of Central Europe, Germany, and the Low Countries

log   book kept on board a ship that records the details of a voyage

Lord Mayor   person in charge of an important city, such as London

Low Countries   name given to the countries of Holland and Belgium

member of Parliament   person who has been voted or appointed to the government of a country

morale   general feelings of optimism and confidence that people have, but can easily lose in moments of stress

mutiny   act of rebelling against orders or against the person or people in command of a ship

nationalism   strong feeling that some people have for their country or nation

navigation   art of finding the right direction when making a journey. Navigation by ship was especially difficult because, for long periods of time, there would be no land to steer by.

New World   name given by Europeans to the lands we now call South, Central, and North America

parish register   record of all births, marriages, and deaths in a parish (district in England), kept in the parish church

patriotic   inspired by devotion to one's country

patriotism   devotion to one's country

pinnace   small boat that could be rowed close to shore or other boats

pirate   someone who robs ships at sea, without government or royal backing

pope   bishop of Rome and head of the Roman Catholic Church

Privy Council   king or queen's private council, made up of the most trusted and reliable members of the government

profit   money or wealth made through business above and beyond what has to be paid out to make the business work

Protestant   Christian faith based on the reforms of the Roman Catholic Church in the early 16th century

realm   kingdom or country with a monarch to rule over it

slave trade   trade in human beings. At the time of Drake, Portuguese, Spanish, and English sailors captured Africans and took them to work as slaves in the Caribbean and South America.

sounding the depth   method of taking a measurement to see how deep the water is, using a sounding line, which has a lead weight on it

Spanish Armada   fleet of armed ships sent by Philip II of Spain in 1588 to invade England

Spanish Main   name given to the Caribbean mainland coast of South America

treasury   part of a government that looks after the monarch and nation's money and general finances

viceroy   governor or head of a colony who acts on behalf of the king or queen

will   document explaining what someone would like to be done with his or her money and belongings after his or her death

Index